Whispers

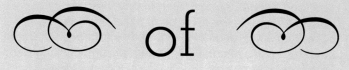 of

Grace

Volume II

Anne de Nada

To order additional copies of this book, contact:
Xlibris
1-888-795-4274
www.Xlibris.com
Orders@Xlibris.com

ISBN: Softcover   978-1-7960-6719-4
         EBook   978-1-7960-6718-7

Print information available on the last page

Rev. date: 10/23/2019

DEDICATION

I dedicate this book to Universal love and light and all that is.
Also, my beloved husband of many cherished years and
my "twin heart" best friend (you know who you are).

ARTIST STATEMENT

Who am I you ask?

I have been a searcher, a traveller and a striver
Seeking my shadow pieces, facets, re-member
Lost fumbling and stumbling, time to let go
Surrender control, fly with the wind
Soaring and spiralling way above the tree tops.

Expansive and free, wild and loving, my truth.
Energetically travelling deep within Mother Earth
Anchoring my light force
Painting golden rainbow colours
Creating a bridge between the two worlds.

FOREWORD

"Voice of the Silent"

This book of art and poetry is a beautiful gift of knowledge from a woman whose passion flows through her written word and paintings. I remember the first time I met Anne, it was in 2009 and for me, a truly a magical time. I had been experiencing mystical dreams and visions since 1995 and each day comprised of astonishing events in a world of synchronicity. I had literally just finished reading an article about a woman known as the Ascended Master Lady Nada, a woman who works from the other side to expand the hearts of humanity, to help us learn unconditional love, and acceptance of the self and others. So you can imagine my surprise when the phone rang, and the person on the other end introduced herself as Anne de Nada - I couldn't help but laugh! Was Lady Nada sending me a physical representative of herself? On looking back on this, I find it quite synchronistic that a woman with a similar name and similar interests to the Ascended Master herself, suddenly appeared right after I had put the book down!

The reason Anne had called me, was to see if she could catch a ride to an event in a nearby town. A group of us were going to see Mother Meera. I had been wanting to meet someone who was considered to be the embodiment of the "Divine Feminine" – and my wish was being granted. Mother Meera was such a person, and she was coming to Kelowna to give a blessing known as "Darshan" which in Sanskrit means "Blessing of the Divine". Of course, we welcomed Anne to join us. Interestingly, I discovered that the word "NADA" means "voice of the silent" and we were about to receive a silent blessing.

As time went on, I grew to know Anne, and discovered that the two of us had many interests in common. We were both artists, we were both on a spiritual path, and we were also very involved in the healing arts. As well, we both loved to travel. Although I have to say, I have never met anyone who has traveled the world quite as much as Anne. Now, after knowing Anne for many years, I can honestly say that she also carries a lot of ideals similar to the Ascended Master Lady Nada as well. Anne's passion to heal people is truly extraordinary, and healing, particularly restoring the balance between the feminine and masculine polarities, is one of Lady Nada's services to humanity. Lady Nada also resonates with all aspects of sound and sound healing, also known as vibrational healing. I know through experience that this is a form of healing Anne also likes to work with.

Anne has poured her very soul into each and every word of this book, and I'm sure that each brush stroke was done with passion and love. I know for a fact that receiving Darshan from Mother Meera that day in 2009 had a huge impact on my life and that my writing took fruition because of it. I can't help but wonder if the same happened for Anne.

I am quite sure that if Anne had a wish for those that are given the opportunity to peruse these books of poetry, it would be for them to receive some sort of healing - for that is what Anne is all about. Like the Ascended Master Lady Nada, Anne's focus is on sharing the qualities of healing and truth, love and compassion, devotion, and selfless service to others.

Mari Sue Baga, Artist also known as Rosaline Temple, Author

Mystic – Divine Revelations, Celestial Visions & Sacred Knowledge

The Swan Stargate 22:22 A Diamond Heart Activation

"Healing arrives on a Whisper"

Whispers of Grace couldn't have a more apt title - each poem captivates the reader with Divine beauty and emotion, a vital connection to ourselves and all that surrounds us. Be prepared to have your thoughts stretched and to be deeply moved in your heart as you absorb the gift in each poem. One can only marvel at the artistry and freedom seen in each brush stroke of Anne's paintings; every colour and nuance plunging the beholder into the depth of yet another reality.

It has truly been an honour for me to meet and come to know the creator of this treasure trove book: Anne de Nada. Freely sharing her wisdom, insights and her love, one cannot help but become devoted to her bright soul. Honestly, I think she may be a nymph herself! It's inspiring to hear her engage in healing work of any sort; always teaching, coaxing an opening, forging a path of release, soothing and comforting with every fibre of her being.

Whispers of Grace is no exception as it also, truly is, a manifestation of healing.

Linda Schopf

Healer, Writer, Vocalist

PREFACE/INTRODUCTION

Poems stream effortlessly through me and I feel so blessed. I watch in amazement as the magic of the words fly across the paper from the nymph world. It is a great joy to live in their presence as each word has its own nymph and they have a past, present and future life. They actually evolve, pass over and everything in between. It is my belief that each word has a life of its own, a beautiful sound within their changing outer landscape and a wonderful essence evolving with time and beauty via their meanings.

This book is the power of miracles orchestrated from my soul's energy - I am in awe of this. While failing English for 10 years straight, never in my wildest dreams would I ever have considered that poems would flow through me. It is with the greatest gratitude that I thank the spirit of Mother Earth and all those bounties she bestows upon us.

These poems were written to be shared with all those searchers and seekers travelling through life's journeys.

ACKNOWLEDGEMENTS

The fruition of this book would not have been possible without the passion and knowledge of Linda Schopf. In deep appreciation, I will be forever grateful for her love and support.

I would like to thank Roselyne Rheaume of Harbour City Imagery and Stephanie of Stephanie Lauren Photography for their dedication and patience in capturing my art pieces photographically.

In conclusion, I wish to thank all those who have given me inspiration, acknowledgement and assistance throughout my journey as a poet. I thank my deceased husband, my best friend, children and travelling companions for their inspiration, guidance and support for my inner growth. Nature so readily has held me in her bosom while I sat and words flowed For this I am humbly grateful.

CONTENTS

SECTION I- ANIMALS

Water Snake

I stood on the rocky edge of the lake,
Transfixed by arrow-like ripples spreading
Over the water's still surface.
Perfect ripples followed from the snake's wake-
A beautiful picture in slow motion.

Never before had I seen a water snake.
Its thick, slender, sleek body gliding
Just below the water's surface.
I knew the rest of the world stood still
While I entered the water snake's world.

Life became so clear to me.
It is not the beginning or the end that matters-
It is how we travel while finding our way.
It's what we leave behind in our wake.
Can we create effortlessly?
Can we glide with grace and spirit?
Releasing life's pure magic?

Universal wisdom is for all to see.
You, water snake,
Opened my eyes and
Burst my heart wide open.

Patience

Camels

Standing tall, proud, and grand
Easily bending, kneeling to the ground
Patient and wise, eyes opening and closing
Aware of all going on.

Never a threat to small children
Or adults under foot,
Gentle, agile, and magnificent
Beast of burden, willing to race for sport.
Star of the northern desert festival.

Adorned with beads, pearls, and buttons
In intricate carpet patterns,
Displaying all heavenly rainbow colours,
Tassels, chains, bells, and whistles.
Celebrating the magic carpet
Riding through life.

Fierce Support & Care

Elephants in India

Hardworking, sturdy, and strong:
A human transportation system up the mountain.
Jostling, massaging, rocking, and rolling us.
Occasionally, blowing your horn for
Reasons unknown to us.

Trunks, ears, and foreheads
Decorated with intricate patterns, shapes, and colours.

Your eyes so compassionately touching our souls,
You are a magnificent creature,
Lost from your home,
Owned by the Indian government.
There are many of you.
My heart yearns for your return home.

Asha's World

Butterfly

Oh, butterfly, butterfly, how do you fly?

Opening and closing as you go.

Down your centre, the origin of your cocoon--

Tremendous upheaval and transformation undergone

To become a truly delicate and gentle

Creature of freedom and beauty.

Oh, butterfly, butterfly, where are you from?

Opening and closing as you do.

Never a threat to anything or being.

Truly spun, direct from the universe.

Maybe that's why you are a pure soul,

Waiting upon the flowers before re-incarnating.

Oh, butterfly, butterfly where are you going?

Opening and closing as God's pure angel.

Land and Sky Union

HERONS

Feathers outstretched like angel wings
Flying high, soaring, dipping, and diving
Riding the sky with grace and purpose
Feeling the joy of being alive.

Standing by the water, king of the sky
Resting with flocks nearby on trees
Exercising branches with feather weights
Scanning your kingdom while basking in sun
Ducks below flap in the breeze.

Parklands stretching far a field
Large animals off in the distance
Antelope, deer, buffalo, and tigers
Freely roaming in God's given land
Called India.

SECTION II- PLANTS, PLACES & NATURE

TREES

Standing tall, sturdy and grand,
Branches, stretching high to the sky,
Roots reaching long, deep and wide-
Penetrating through rocks, over
Boulders, climbing, burrowing below.

Patient and wise their gifts unseen,
Sign posts directing earth's energy flow
From dawn to sunset, delivering O_2
Our elixir of life.

True magic lies within your trunk,
As trillions of energetic bubbles
Ride up and down your core,
Connecting, communicating, carrying
Offerings of healing, wisdom and love.

Simple pleasures are free.
Lean up against a tree,
Extend your loving arms-
And receive immeasurable
Blessings, healings, energy and love

Mexican Soul Tree

Cactus

A true creator
Rising from dust-
A master of protrusion and expansion,
Fearless and wise.

Prickly, delicate, commanding respect
Your deepest secrets
Protected within your honeycomb,
Conserving precious droplets,
Teaching us to waste not.

You send forth youthful adventurers
Whose shoots grow, mature,
Generously supporting
New generations of beauty and grace.

Within you, beloved Cactus,
Time, Space, and Movement
Grow eternal.

Butterfly Jungle Community

SUNFLOWERS GOLDEN

Sunflowers of all kinds are open hearts
Especially the sunflowers which are golden
They invite all eyes to peer and search
Into the centre of their beauty

Oh, flower expand and caress
All hearts and eyes peering forth
Butterflies alight upon you briefly
In moments of truth and beauty
Knowing the wisdom of openness

As the sun sets and it is time to close
And repose for another day
All of heaven's wisdom is contained
Within your simple opening and closing.

Microscopic Wonder

NATURE, MINISCULE & GIGANTIC

Twisted, contorted roots
Strung across the foot path
Hardy and grounded
In between fine, soft, dried pine needles.

Baby spruce trees spreading
Their wings;
Tall pine trees not so well.

Sun's magic gifting rays,
Warmth, and beams,
Lighting the fire in my heart.

Oh, butterfly, butterfly
How magnificent your home.
Beneath my feet a dragonfly
Flutters, sunning and resting on a leg.

Above:
The rock escarpment lining the Nahanni gorge.
A triangle rock, rising up from
The middle of the torrent
Carved through eons by water power
Tunnelling, funnelling temple steps below.

Smashing, thrashing, tumbling
Rumbling north to the Arctic.
Roaring, chaotic, hustling and bustling
Forming mist, flying high.

All around, rushing, gushing topsy-
Turvy water explosions.

Shouting out, sounding high and low,
I am here, admire my magnificent force.

A mist above the falls captures
A mystical rainbow beauty.

Bountiful Tree

Amongst the trees, colourful mushrooms sprout
White, brown, orange, and yellow.

Red cranberries, shining through
Pale, dark, lime green leaves.

Yellow buttercups open wide
Different textures, shapes and shadows.

For all our astonishments
These are my Heavenly Delights.

Flow of the Cosmos

DIVINE MOTHER

She knows and loves us like no other,
From deep within her being.
She is the beginning and end of love.
Her wisdom rises, flows up and out
From within her core, then all about.

She spreads her love like the divas with each word
Observing the many languages, rhythms, and voices.
Her earthly children play, tumble, and fumble,
Laughing and smiling under her protective umbrella.

We surrender our pain and sorrows to her,
Rejoice with her through our thoughts, feelings, and actions.
She is the grace that flows in and around our hearts' spaces--
Without her we are nothing.

Separation from her grace and kindness
Sends arrows of pain and terror deep within;
Lost, we struggle to return to her bosom,
Where all is forgotten, forgiven, and embraced.

She raises us up from our earthly home
And enlightens us with earthly beauty.
Her loving eyes, forever present,
Fill us with her divinity.

Fluidity

POWERFUL WIND AROUND THE ISLAND

Wind has a voice,
Has a force,
Reaches everywhere.

It roars in long sentences,
Paragraphs, and stories,
Nothing is untouched by its presence.
Its voice rises to high pitches and sinks to
short notes, like small white caps.

Dancing branches, swaying fronds,
Feeling cozy, safe behind glass doors.
Mother Nature's symphony of dance and music.
No escaping its presence,
It cleans up all loose ends.

It tests trees, plants, and grasses
In ferocious challenges.
Wave upon wave travelling to shore
Grey clouds above, forewarning impending storms.

Listen to her roar, roar, and roar:
I am nature's cleaner
Lots to say, I come after the calm
Before the storm and sometimes during.

My power demands respect.
Not as powerful as fire,
Man becomes humbled
As I circulate decay upon the ground:
Recycling for soil and new growth.

I ENHANCE THE CIRCLE OF LIFE.

Meditating Energy

Water

Sliding
    Gliding
        Slithering down
            Smooth rock inclines

Still
    Gentle
        Shimmering
            Moonlit lakes

Drips
    Drops
        Snowing
            Ice crystals, hailstones

Falling from above
    Ice bergs
        Crunching
        Crashing
           Smashing
            Rising from below

Gentle ripples
    Among the reeds
        Lapping, slapping
        Swaying, cradling
            Baby Moses

Waves
    Floating
        Tumbling
        Rumbling
        Onto shore

Water
    The matrix of life
        Sustaining, supporting
        Teeming with nourishment
        Billions and trillions of
            Expressions of spirit

While our waterless friends
    Rocks, deserts, sand dunes, mountains
        Sustain eons of wisdom

Gentleness

Earth

Full of heart, is Mother Earth
Offering her love to all.
Nourishment, shelter, and protection
Live by her universal truths.
Treat others as
They wish to be treated.
Abundance is for the asking.

Earth is the ultimate creator;
Her soils, skies, waters, and mountains
All teeming with millions,
Trillions, of organisms.
An infinity of life.
Ever changing cloud forms
Flowing, streaming, streaking,
Billowing across her horizons.
Always, even as we sleep.

She exhibits the gentlest of creatures,
Plants and wind to massage all her beings.
When matter falls from the sky
She accepts and embraces another mountain.
When her tummy rumbles
We all hear her call.
We see her molten lava flow,
Freezing in time a civilization.

Her gravity supports us all,
Her day and night turns set our clocks,
Her rhythmical seasons caress us.
We rake her hair with autumn leaves;
We swim in her still, blue summer lakes.
We glide and slide and ski her curves in winter,
Splash and jump in her tears of joy in spring.

Cambodian Nut Tree

She never abandons us,
Though we might her.
Her love is constant.
She never criticizes or judges.
Like the Grand Canyon,
Her patience is breathtaking.

Her wisdom arises after the calm
Of thunder and lightning storms.
All there ever is, is love--
Love is to evolve and let us evolve
On revolving, evolving Mother Earth.

Flowers in the Dark

AFRICA

Africa, Africa:
land of far horizons
upon far horizons
stretching to infinity
We came searching for the spirit of the wild
We found Mother Earth's creatures living in harmony with man
Oh, what a wonderful sight to watch
two leopards feasting on their kill
not two minutes old
of a wildebeest.

To see the elephants mate with their tusks
To see a large colony of baboons frolicking
Mothers with young on their backs
or clinging underneath their bellies
To see the giraffes, the stilt walkers of the savanna
To see the delicate spirit of the bush buck
minding his harem of 50 does.

To watch the Maasai herdsmen
dressed in colourful garments
tending their flocks
of goats and cattle
To share in the afternoon walk to the water hole
with two male lions and then nearby
to discover a lioness and her two young cubs
frolicking on the ground and rolling in the tall grass
Oh, what a wonderful gift.

Like the bush buck whose spirit I longed to touch
before I could
I needed to know
just how close I could move.

The artist in us is crying out for expression
It challenges us to travel into the wilderness of our souls
to sit in the bumpy Land Rover
waiting to be at the right spot at the right time
Will our hearts burn to make handicrafts or lace
fly a plane or sail a boat
Once we have lit the pilot of our hearts
the journey begins and all else follows

Alternate Beauti-verse

ISLAND

Oh, how I dream
To be marooned on a tropical island
On the other side of the world

The beat of the heart
The heat of the sand
The sound of lapping waves
The smell of salty air
Have more meaning than
The ticking of any clock

For guidance, entertainment, and light
The bright shining stars at night
Reward my attention and devotion
By shooting across the sky
Like passing star ships homeward bound

Crabs and sand bites
Seaweed and sea shells
Coconut husks and volcanic pumice
All litter the morning beach

The seagulls and larks
The moon and sun above
Peering out to the horizon
Watching the sea and sky
Bless this island paradise

Nymph World

NAHANNI RIVER

River, river speak to me
Steady babbling brooks as you flow
Rumbling and tumbling as you go
Resisting naught as you fly by.

The main transportation system
For thrill seekers, Megan and Mary,
Happy when catching air
Then landing with a thud.

Life support for bears--
Black, brown, and grizzly--
Rafters and canoeists flowing by,
Happy as larks, not falling in.

All in awe of high mountains,
Library cliffs, rock scree,
Steep gorges, cavernous canyons.
Hikers rising early for physical challenges.

Team work, digging ditches,
Unloading rafts, establishing kitchens.
Groaning, sating meals by Liam
For exultant, famished adventurers.

Virgin forests, panoramic views,
Pale, medium blue skies,
One day cumulous clouds, the next smoke.
Man loves comparisons and extremes.

River of life teaching us
Sometimes to expand, or to slow down.
Others times, to narrow the focus
To flow swiftly, to enjoy the ride.

This is my heavenly paradise
Here on Earth.

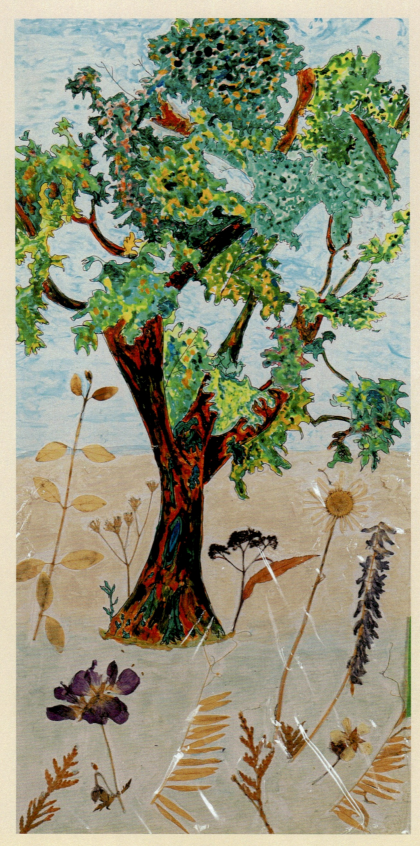

Wisdom & Comfort

TRAVELLERS

Travellers know a freedom unknown to others.
They become impervious to chaos;
Underneath there is a knowing that
All is possible when following one's heart.

Sometimes they are required to turn on a dime,
Accepting others' customs, cultures, and foods
In the continuous smorgasbord of life.

Travellers are open, living by the grapevine.
Knowledge is constantly updated and invaluable.
There is a common language, no matter the different tongues.
All are guided by trust and an adventurous spirit.

Some love cities, shops, and entertainment;
Others love ashrams, monasteries, and temples.
Still others seek the inner wisdom and peace
Of lakes, mountains, forests, rivers, and the sea.

The price is disconnection from family and friends,
Careers, financial stability, and ancestral community.

Like the prodigal son, there is a time to return
To the warmth and caring of home fires;
To safety and security that comes with roots
Renewed and revitalized with well nurtured wanderlust.

Printed in the United States
By Bookmasters